The Problem with Solitaire
(Is That It Can Be Hard to Tell
If You're Playing Yourself)

☙

Lucia Misch

Write Bloody North

writebloodynorth.ca

First edition.
ISBN: 978-0-9920245-6-7

Cover Design by Derrick Brown
Interior Layout by Winona León
Edited by Alessandra Naccarato
Proofread by Stuart Ross
Author Photo by A. Schlechtleitner
Cover photo: Hollis Linschoten

Type set in Bergamo from www.theleagueofmoveabletype.com

Write Bloody North
Toronto, ON

Support Independent Presses
writebloodynorth.ca

for Chicken, of course

THE PROBLEM WITH SOLITAIRE
(IS THAT IT CAN BE HARD TO TELL
IF YOU'RE PLAYING YOURSELF)

THE PROBLEM WITH SOLITAIRE
(IS THAT IT CAN BE HARD TO TELL
IF YOU'RE PLAYING YOURSELF)

♥

♦

I AM WORRIED THAT THE ANSWERS I WAS BORN WITH HAVE LONG SINCE RUBBED AWAY

If there is a new place on this body—
an undiscovered patch of skin concealed

somewhere on my surface, as yet unhandled
—I would like it to show itself now.

I've turned keys under my tongue and combed my scalp
for passageways. I wrote *OPEN SESAME* on the mirror,

tried unfamiliar trips hoping to scrape a knee I never had,
but all I've done is scour the familiar sore.

Maybe this place waits like Brigadoon
—emerges from my mist

once every hundred years—
hoping no hunters stumble past.

Maybe there's a spell I have to say perfectly
to make it appear. Maybe this is it: the plea

that will produce the kept secret, the wardrobe
my questions can climb through to the hidden realm

where I am complete as a snowfall
that no one has yet woken up under.

WHO KNOWS WHAT HE THINKS OF ME NOW?

A calendula petal unfurling in acid. The bite taken out of Bikini Atoll.
Some spider who built her web across the doorway of his memoir, maybe

a velvet box with a snap-up lid, corners worn naked in his pocket.
In that rounded room, small as an apology tucked among roses, I must wait

as he remembers: a silhouette against the headboard
eating underdone crumb cake with my glasses off,

short-sighted like he liked me, the light having to slide through
his blinds to find my hair, pinned in magnificent spirals to the wall.

I was supposed to be a suitcase large enough for a long journey,
full of clothes that show—wherever the whistle blows—who he believes

himself to be. Is this how I go missing from my own portrait?
Become a vanished lump of sugar that makes his coffee

the way he doesn't drink it? The once-favourite cufflink
resented for letting go, responsible for having been lost?

I make it my work to recall him as he was:
outlined in reasons to leave, his hands up my skirt,
against the car, his own name pouring from his mouth.

WHAT I TOOK FROM MY MOTHER

A name: my second middle, or my first last.

A distaste for underwires and a light
blue bra, when she was done with it.

The habit of arranging small objects
into altars, readying every room
for an offering.

A long-necked ease with earrings.

A list of Nevers:
> let your host do the dishes.
> forget to write a thank you note.
> use soap on the wooden bowl
> or metal on the Teflon.
> stay with a man who hits you
>> no matter if your best necklace is on the nightstand.
>> no matter if every coat you own is hung in his closet.
>> no matter what he says, it will never only happen once.

Bad vision, swimming lessons.

Her youngest daughter.
> I'm sorry. I meant to be more careful,
> but left too many pieces of that girl
> in places I'd been warned not to return to.

THE PROBLEM WITH SUBJECT–OBJECT DISAGREEMENT

I am cranky at the Musée d'Orsay.

Just half an hour in,
already sick of regarding
my own image, framed and lit,
or in cases of museum glass
designed to minimize reflection.

The café coffee is bullshit
in both quality and cost
and my back hurts, my hips
are cramped, uterus sore.

I had an IUD implanted yesterday,
a special kind that isn't approved back home.

When I got up to dress
in the gyno's small office,
I'd left fresh strokes of blood
across the end of the doctor's table:
a composition we have made
—or have been made to make—
since doctors, since tables, began.

In the Musée's downstairs bathroom,
I change my pad, wash my hands,
meet my own glare in the mirror.
On impulse, lift my shirt.
Under it, a thousand years
of stone and oil paint arranged
in the arcs with which men
like to tell their myths,
express their gifts.

I leave before getting my money's worth,
walk through the museum shop
without buying a postcard
or any other reproduction
of some overpriced object.

FIGURING OUT, IN RETROSPECT,
HOW MANY TIMES IT MIGHT HAVE COUNTED

When I said *I don't want to*
and he heard *try to make me*

he put his fingers in
and noted
that my head tilted
back
and stomach rose
mouth began to open

so he pointed out
I was being a hypocrite

a reasoning that seemed
unassailable.

I didn't downplay it
later
didn't think
to mention it at all

    already open jeans
    the couch
    his logic

already folded
into how I thought
this was all supposed to go.

BRAZEN BULL

I.

There is nothing to be done,
my friend tells me, about the scalpels
that dervish in her hips.
They don't wear dull
but hone themselves on bone.
She is a whetstone,
every movement sharpening.

At night, when the vice is tightest,
she wedges into bed and sways
between the splinter on the left
and the splinter on the right.
She dreams she's eating thistles.

You should have drawn today,
the thistles say.

II.

In ancient Sicily, a device for public execution
was invented: a hollow sculpture of a bull
forged of brass. The condemned was locked inside
and a fire lit under its belly.

In the bull's throat a system of tubes twisted
so that screams, otherwise inaudible,
came to the gathered crowd as a gentle bellow.

When the door was pried open,
the victim's bones shone
like opals in the ash.

They could be sifted out, it's said,
and strung together for jewellery.

III.

My friend spreads thumbtacks on her toast.
Takes her dagger for a walk. Milk's gone off,
so she has her coffee two ounces lighter.
Her brother just married an hour in a folding chair.
Her friends play in a folk punk threshold.

She says she thought there would be something
waiting on the other side of Pain, who moved in
and started to redecorate without asking.

Once enough hardwood was replaced
with wall-to-wall wasps, once the coat hooks
turned to thumbscrews, the vases to grenades,
an insight was supposed to emerge,
some exquisite sting to make her grateful
for the difficult decor.

But the blacksmith who wrought her
forgot to put a trombone in her throat.
No algorithm of air there
turns shriek to song,
and the onlookers cover their ears,
turn away unsatisfied, saying,

This is the most pointless execution
we've ever seen.

THE PROBLEM WITH PRONOUN–VERB AGREEMENT

We have drunk. Instead. Again.
And we have eaten pizza
and thrown it back toward the plate.
The two-fingered pitch, curveless ball,
constant umpire proclaiming *Out*.

Now we are headed home to lose
at solitaire on our iPod until sleep
sends us to another morning of sucking it in
and arching our back before the mirror,
the mirror arching back.

Until then we will play the cards
on top of each other
until there are no pairings left.

We are tired of having our ass
handed to us at solitaire. We are tired
of handing our ass to ourself.

We ought to take our girlfriend home,
to where the grit on the floor is
familiar, and slide our cheek up her thigh
until the wolf spiders know we live here,
the flies stop hatching around us.

Hold her through an entire species' life cycle.
Weeks at least. However long it takes
to blur into a different restive body.

EVERY INJURY I'VE EVER HAD

Makes me feel less temple,
more school of dead jellyfish
packed in trash bag,
half an earthworm
stuck to shovel head,
corn dog in condom of skin.

It has been suggested
that when I long to be peeled,
am repulsed by the landfill feeling
of breath,

I should face a mirror
and say:

> *Body, you are beautiful.*
> *You are strong. You are enough.*
> *Thank you, for everything you do for me.*

> (Sounds like some patronizing bullshit,
> and my body, god knows,
> gets enough of that without my help.)

No advice has been offered,
however, regarding
what spell I might speak
to reconcile
the bandoliers of severed fingers
that I must dress each morning
to the naked creature
they are strapped around.

I'll have to figure it out myself:
how to convene
this congregation of the susceptible,
make of it a meal,

call my body to the table
set with its own disfigured feast,
and order: *Eat.*
> *This is your only chance*
> *to be filled.*
> *You are the only executioner*
> *allowed in the delivery room.*
> *The only archivist*
> *who will burn her life's work.*

What else can I do?

This curdle between us,
my self and its form,
is just the way of one
wanting thing
tied inside a different
wanting thing.

So be it. My body is a child
who shrieks
from the seat of the shopping cart.

So be it. My body breaks dishes
into the sink and screams
that it didn't ask to be born.

One day we will both be Alexandria.
Whatever collection of tiny scrolls
I amass will not outlast its walls.
Our fights will end

with us back in each other:
deflated, soft, panting
as one punctured lung.

DIGESTION BEGINS IN THE MOUTH

Part of my motivation for doing it
was so that no one else would have to.

—Rachael Denhollander

So that
    eyes can leave the ceiling,
    stop recounting cracks

So that
    the irregular bones shown
    through the skin of an ankle
    a stomach, a success,
    are revealed: vertebrae
    all along, so disturbing
    with their pedicles, laminae
    processes   jutting so

    that no one imagined
    the spine they might
    articulate when joined

So that
    teeth can lift from tongue
    fists release back into fingers

So that
    the palm reader will not
    gasp
      push the money back
    and refuse
      for any price
    to say what she has seen
    in the crescents cut
    across the life lines

So that when all is done
the courtroom will be empty,

cleared like a path
leading away from her answer.

ON THE FIRST DAY: LIGHT

Copper sheen, hint of dawn
stamped between my thighs.

By morning,
I am new shore, my crux
the border between the land
from which blood runs
and the water it rejoins.

Waistbands snap line
between sea and sky;
horizon pressed across hip bones.

Disinclined to be a fruit tree
who yields fruit
after its kind,

I let seeds
go empty to the earth.

I never once say *let there be*,

will not make myself
a moon
or bring forth
abundantly moving
creatures that hath life.

Instead, I am the fortunate sort of god
who gets to choose against creation.

I NEVER THINK OF MY LIFE AS ANYTHING OTHER THAN SOMETHING THAT WILL END WHEN I DIE

Well, almost never. Sometimes I think of it
as that dress at the thrift store that fits so sharp
I turn and turn in the mirror, too enchanted
by the waist it creates to check if I can sit down.

The fabric is so thick, I have to push the needle
with a pair of pliers. I find a thread in my mouth
every morning that must be put back through the eye
to darn the day that waits.

> *People aren't wired to make choices*
> *based on long-term consequence,* I say,
then wet the stripe of glue across my tongue,
wed it to paper, summon fire, light another smoke.

I'd love to cushion my choices by promising half of them heaven,
sucker-punch Loss with a handful of *we'll-all-meet-again*
loading my blow. But what I can't know I don't consider
to be one of the pattern pieces.

There's a billboard near my house that says
WHEN YOU DIE YOU WILL MEET GOD.
So I could be wrong.

Maybe should assume I am, and put my money
on the invisible horse who will only become real,
rearing from the gate on silver hooves,
if he is the winning bet.

EACH TWO, THEIR OWN

To relax, my girlfriend likes to go to spas in fancy hotels,
be massaged with salts and oil, steamed like a bok choy.

I prefer bars with bad lighting, to get drunk
and yell my secrets at anyone who won't remember them.

Though we loosen different, we wind up the same:
          handfuls of muscle pulled in our shoulders and sides,
          strangers leaning into pressure points,
dead skin scrubbed off by salves that sting the cuts.

WE ARE EXPERTS IN EACH OTHER'S
BENT INGREDIENTS

She comes to me naked with grief, hung up
in the harsh, knowing light of last year,

steps into the shower, her face slipping
under hands gloved in sud, the day

lathered off with hotel soap, flicks of liner
at the crests of her lids rubbed grey in the mask of emulsion.

She can purr comets from the bed
of a borrowed pickup truck,

old ice falling from her mouth
a slow snow on the lakeshore.

I whisk cream under her skirt,
one finger twirling the breeze there,

an agitation of satin in the passenger seat.
There are pressed flowers between her moans,

petals that give up rosewater
when her throat wrings my name.

As she sleeps, her fists uncurl; I see words
printed across the soft parts of her stroke.

They read, without relent:
there is work to be done.

Every morning is a fray we plunge our bodies,
odd and made-up, into. At the end of the day

we find scintillas of effort
in the aftermaths of our beauty:

mascara twilights cast under lashes,
red tracks round our waists when we tug off tights.

Blisters gather at our heels,
the consequence of skin defying its containment.

INTENDER

You decide
at first
to be brazen:
a different
kind of girl

tits out to prove
you've got no place
to carry an apology

peeing in the alley
behind the bank
in broad daylight

yelling across the table
how everyone should
learn to put on condoms
with our mouths

the same way
you'd say
we should all know
how to change a tire.

It's choice
not instinct
to spit shame back
at any eyes it can sting

to act unembarrassed
when you still are.

And as you strip
and piss and shout

sure you'll never
actually feel
the way you behave
        about your breasts
        and leg hair, the wet
        spot and smell of blood
        streaked on stomach
you become
in quiet
one of your own
naked beliefs.

CICATRICES

I.

In October, when I was fifteen,
a gust of wind ruffled the cookbook,
turned it to a secret page.

I read how Pain
is the egg in the cake,
binding all other ingredients.

Afraid I could forget the recipe,
I copied it down myself
in irrevocable ink,
my handwriting
changed: N no longer
had legs, O
could no longer
balance on its own.

It was necessary:
            that everything be linked
            by the dark lines
            I believed only I could see.

II.

It's obvious now,
that common knowledge
would make
an unsatisfying secret.

Obvious:
> don't have to meet me
> at a calligraphy class
> or an arm-wrestling match,
> offer a shake
> or throw a stapler at my face
> *(think fast)*, to figure out
> which hand I write with.

III.

So if you want to read me,
go on, look away
and so will I,
make a show
of studying the horizon,
busy my face in the wind
while you scan the lines.

It can be hard
to know which eye
to watch
which eye to admire,
but like I said
you can
look,
it's what I'd do.

After all:
       what would a dog, so obsessed
       with her own buried bones,
       try to read in the eyes of other dogs
       except where their own bones might be buried?

COMING HOME, SAN JOSÉ I

Weird how someone's life
can change forever so slowly.

Elaine said that once,
while another DUI arrest
went down in the parking lot
of the all-night pie diner.

It just dragged on forever,
like they always had
—all those cops
milling around—
and there we were,
nothing to do
but watch over meringue.

We were back for Winter Break
by this point, older than we'd ever been
before. Could've just gone to a bar
except that someone always has to drive.

DIORAMA: FROM THE GREEK "TO SEE THROUGH"

Our basement smells like the inside
of a winter hat: sweat-damp wool, Clairol, scalp.
Wet jeans ring off the walls of the dryer
as we pass the bong between mildewed couches,
feet on glass-top coffee table, a strewn ashtray mess.

The pot makes me cough like a jammed doorbell.
I hate the way it turns water dusty and tannic,
how I chew my lips to splinters
no matter how many times I go for my Chapstick.

But that is the price of admission
to the museum where I can give our Tuesday afternoon
the reverent attention that teachers told us to reserve
for someone else's wonders.

If I get high enough, I can see
every smashed roach and beer can,
blanket and combat boot,
as artifacts of an era
worth careful conservation.

I will marvel
that of all the other
engraved Zippos and second-hand amps,
teenage stoners' early-aughts sweaters
and ugly upholstery,
some curator deemed *ours* exemplary,
brought us together
in deliberate tableau.

If this tendency
to venerate their random crap
makes me a socially weird
and inexplicably emotional
person to get baked with,
my friends don't seem to mind.

The visiting hours are loose here:
I can probably even crash if I need to,
so I study—their keychains,
their crushed packs of Camels,
someone's brother's pet lizard—

for as long as it takes
to find myself back
on the other side of the glass.

A CORNER   SO MEANINGLESS
SHOULD NOT BE   TURNED ALONE

so fine	that we find each other
every New Year's	home
here	in the slab backyard
where the boys	(always only the boys)
play tetherball	swinging in fits
and spins	the ball straining
to be off its chain	cuts the exact orbit
in the crowd	as last time round
this is a city	that has been
throwing the same	three house parties
for decades	so there's forever
been someone drunk	cajoling someone
drunker	with a slice of bread
in a bathroom	missing the countdown
starting another loop	without being
aware that the last one	just ended

ENOUGH

I found this man in a kitchen once:
freckles strewn like shells
across shooting-range shoulders,
a scar stretched like a waking cat
across one arm. He looked sweet
and sharp as rye and ginger.
I decided I would take him,
and I took him.

I was nineteen, with no idea
how a body can misplace
the meaning of *enough*.

He was strong as a door frame, kind,
well-read, and full of dirty electricity.

He'd roll expired bus transfers,
make ridges of cocaine
vanish from my nightstand,
then lower himself back into bed.

I'd watch ten thousand tiny match heads
strike inside him, his pupils swell
like broken fingers,
freckles skitter and skip,
flecks of oil in a hot skillet.
He smelled of lightning strike
setting rubber on fire,
of sexy little bullet factory.
The defibrillators in his fingers
ran their current up my thighs.

I didn't think to mind;
we were keeping each other company,
he and I, in the difference
between not caring
and just being careless.

Years later, a friend told me
that German has no word for *addict*.
Instead, the person who cannot stop
grinding himself to powder
is called a *seeker*.

I understood,
had felt it through those freckles:
the charge incurred by searchers

that a lost electron must hunt
for an atom to balance

how an arc desperate for ground
will burn through anyone it touches.

MY GRANDMOTHER SAW
THE TERRACOTTA SOLDIERS
ON HER TRIP TO CHINA

How long ago was that? I ask,
eating almonds on her couch.

Oh, it must have been five years by now.

But I was grown then too.
If that was five years,
I can hold the last decade
in one hand like a ham sandwich.

When my hands were so much
slighter than a slice of bread, it would've
seemed impossible to palm time like this.

My grandmother is holding almost ten
ham sandwiches.

Was it cool? I ask.

It was madness, she says.
It was mobbed.

*You had to fight to the railing
just to look into the pit.*

PALIMPSEST

After the stroke, my grandfather
was a palimpsest in a high-backed chair.
When dinner was done, he'd look up,
effaced, ask what had been for dinner.

   Look at what's left,
my grandmother would tell him.

Scraps of gristle and a trace of green:
lamb with mint jelly.
Mayo smears, a round bone:
pork chops and coleslaw.

Then she'd clear the plates,
give the scraps to the spaniels.

★

   Even people have tides,
my father told me
on a beach in Puget Sound.

   *It's easier to see
   in a body of water,
   but we're pulled too,*

   a tiny bit taller twice a day.

★

With my tide kept high,
the things I've lost
are just gone things.

But when the waves wash out,
what I forget rises and darkens.

>The pointless shapes of parties
>where we girls learned to dance like snakes
>while gin thickened in the freezer.

>The ebb and flow of thirst.

>The gallons of shame I can squeeze
>from half a lemon of misstep.

>That eventually I'll have to quit.

>>That one's like an inherited harmonica:
>>wrapped up in tissue, waiting to be learned.

THREE ACTS

I.

I joke that if it weren't for crushing mental illness,
I'd never see the inside of a gym.

I like to credit my existential incompetence
with what little upper-body strength I have.
I think it's funny, and keeps people
from seeing me as weak.

Ryan suggests we swim.
When I don't answer, he puts my shoes on for me,
packs a bag with our suits and towels, the blue ones,
still too new to have been roughed in the wash.
He steers me to the car, a hand on each of my shoulders.

On the way to the community centre
I start to cry at a red light.

> *I want to be able to be other parts of me,* I say.
> *I'm just so bored by this.*

He reaches over, strokes my arm, says,

> *Hey, the pool will be warm,*
> *and things always feel lighter in the water.*

But we've left the bag at home,
must retrace our steps,
retrace them again.

Stopped at the same red light I say,

> *It's okay.*
> *It's good when things take too long.*
> *It means more time I've lived*
> *and less I'll have to.*

Ryan starts to laugh, takes a hand off the bag,
touches my shoulder. *Oh man*, he says,

the silver lining is always the most depressing part.

II.

Ryan jokes that my sadness
only seems to sit well with me
if I think no one can see it.

       Yeah, I say.
       Otherwise how will I know
       it's not just performance?

He hands me tea I didn't ask for,
steeped on our small stove.

       But isn't hiding it a performance too?

I wouldn't make the effort
of tea for myself, would rather not
notice any ailments it might aid.

Rather not have to ask
if this hard day is just a hard day

or the bell that starts
another round of the fight,
calls me back to belt out
one more act of this ugly opera

in a theatre built to resound best
when the house is empty.

III.

And lo! I have left *The Joy Of Cooking*
open to cornbread on the table.

And lo! I have left the butter out to soften and spoil,
run its foil and shine the black glass atop the stove.

And lo! I have left the kitchen to go read in the messy bedroom,
an article about Belgian euthanasia for the terminally depressed.

Earlier, Ryan and I walked to the park up the road, sat against some roots.
I watched the moment where they dive and disappear into the dirt;

he twisted sticks to standing in the frozen ground.
Back home, he took off my boots and rolled my heels under his knuckles,

kneading that place that takes the first weight of every step,
then moved up to my calves, his hands inquiring

as to the shape and soreness of the muscles there,
while I thought about internet searches for *common overdose drugs*

or over-the-counter overdose drugs, not making a plan, exactly,
but handling the dark fantasy of a plan, inquiring as to its shape and soreness.

I've set it down, for now, to wash the dishes while the cornbread cools.
They will be put away by one of us tomorrow, or lo! left out for several days.

THE PROBLEM WITH BEING REASSURED I'M NOT LAZY (JUST DEPRESSED)

is that
that's exactly
the sort of excuse
a lazy person
would want
(pills for)

is that
I finally got
a microwave
and it turns out
heating/eating
food is still
too much
(work)

is that
I've never
been/done
well enough
to know
(the difference)

MAYBE SHE DIDN'T THINK
                    IT WAS A GOOD TIME
FOR A TENNIS METAPHOR

What the doctor doesn't say
as she writes a prescription
                                        for a new mind
                                            in blue pen
is that the wall I've been playing
against may have made me
                            accustomed to a certain
                                style of opponent.

That a wall will always return
your shot at an angle
                                equal and opposite
                            to the one you gave it
so if the ball splits your lip
you have only your own swing
                                        to blame.

She doesn't warn me
that the wall
                        who can answer to bruised wrist
                            without flinch or apology
may not have prepared me
to play against anyone but myself.

WHAT SIMPLE MACHINE DID WE THINK WE WERE BUILDING BETWEEN US?

Summer

We wrestle on the lawn,
tousle, flush, our joy
pulled to the surface like a blush,
delights tangling together:

a new rigging
a net that will catch but not capture,
a rosary I can lean into.

Fall

I watch old episodes
of *How It's Made*
all day, lie in bed
with lathes, conveyor belts,
industrial origin stories
whirring around me.

You sit, fingers twitching at the keys,
building planets in an elsewhere
where you command armies
with the spasms of your hands.

My moving parts
lock against each other,
bind and tremble.

An inch of water
in a jar on the nightstand
turns to the taste of dust.

Winter

Stitches in the flag
of a conquered country,

levees made of lace:

we are toothless, tiny

neither of us lever enough
to lift the other
back into a bustling heart.

When I realize
that loving each other
does not make us
immune to sorrow

it rips me right in half.

Spring

I can trick myself
to sleep if I measure
my breath against yours,
deepen each draw
until we gather and
let out in rhythm.

For years
we will mend this way:
while at rest,
moving the treadle
together in time,

the teeth
of two gears
who meet and meet,
compel each other forward.

COMING HOME, SAN JOSÉ II

Sometimes, if we were on our way home
real late, Elaine used to stop her Corolla
in the middle of 280 and we'd get out,
stand on the lane lines, leave the doors open,
sit on the trunk to smoke.

I guess we figured
the freeway was so straight
we'd see another car coming
with time to spare,

get back up to speed
before the driver even knew
our tail lights hadn't been moving.

Memory likes to polish its own silver.
Still, it was probably a really stupid thing to do.

I know that, and it doesn't make me sad:

how we were squeezing out of a soft cage
into a small room.

REAL SWAN REBELLION

What to make of it?
The hot breath of extinction
at the nape of each day,
arms of the storm sweeping
our table, decanter
undoing itself upon the land.

The flood came
and there's one coming:
glimmer delivered in cycle,
crystal knocked across
the collar of the world.

Goose grease stains the wallpaper.
A fleur-de-lis starts bleeding with the moon.

There are crossed fingers
breaking behind backs,
television sets circled
in church basements.
Thumbtacks tire
of holding up the veil.

We must know,
for all the nothing
that settles in
between tantrums,
how the clear liquor wind
will shout the sky again

another blast of long-lost
teeth and backhand,
another sudden spate
of fire on the teevee.

There are porcupines
turning themselves inside out
for the sake of mercy,
and guns everywhere.

There are children
pulling ice plant
from the dunes of Monterey,
and drones delivering
the weather.

A real swan rebellion, this time:
glide and muscle, squawk
and great wings
beating the water
as alligators line up
like a runway
for the new engulfing.

Our boat's more
than half hole now,
and doesn't that
just make
the old stigmata buzz.

SEISMOMETER

You can't hear an earthquake coming,
the cat assures me.

He can hear the plans of birds
an alley over, turns his ears
long before their wings
applaud the evening above our yard.

His first-aid kit is not crowded
with flat, packed gauze.
His canned goods are uncounted.

He settles on the piano bench,
each of his counties finding its seat,
soft regions opining
      alright then   in turn.

I listen from bed,
checklisting myself
up one side of rest
and down the other.

The cat comes, thrumming low
and unbroken, settles in beside me.

He understands—with the same whisker intuition
that calls him to my chest during the worst of it—
that all caged creatures pace this way.

When the plates finally sigh together,
the cat will likely be under the hydrangea
where he likes to sit
and not wait
inside himself for sleep.

IN EVENT OF MOON DISASTER

In event of Moon Disaster,
do not think that the lattices you look through
—the screen-door view,
your inebriate insect eyes,
the panes of the calendar—

can be camera obscuras, pinhole vistas
through which to safely watch
the new eclipse slide by. Do not waste
your spit making your lips look wet
when the rash tide comes anyway.

Be unbeholden to the beekeepers,
their careful white costumes.
They believe your spit is honey,
want to crawl into your comb,
curl in a cell of your tidy kaleidoscope,
be an atom in the hive of atoms.

Be ready for the Apple Pickers' Union
to go on general strike. To see women
boosting nude fruit back into trees.
For the sun to lift their dress in solidarity
and dance the fiasco on the trap doors
until your bedfellows in the bomb shelters
kiss you awake to listen.

In event of Moon Disaster,
do not think that we put men in robot bodies
without reason. These careful white coffins
are the smallest Edens
we have ever put an Atom inside of.

Do not think of the panic,
weightless suffocation,
the leader's speech laid like a wreath
of rocks around a helmet.

Do not consider a sailor's funeral,
commitment to the deep.

The lead clothes you wear
in case the bomb drops
are not as heavy as you think.

Do not think
of distance, dismay, dark matters.

Think instead of your children,
with their heads under their desks.
The smell of coffee burning
re-entry into the kitchen.
The initials pocket-knifed
on the bus window, steady
as a footprint in dust.

Think instead of the strike breaking,
apple juice returning to the shelves.
How sure it would feel
to be stockpiling.

See how the screen-door hinges need oiling?
And the wood-glue sticks like reason again,
and the lipstick tastes like need.

THUNDER IS THE NEW NIGHT OUT

The guys yucking it up on morning radio
are losing their shit for a living:

> *So get this get this, there's this*
> *new study says kids, says KIDS*
> *shouldn't shoot each other*
> *with nerf guns anymore. So what*
> *are they supposed to shoot each other*
> *WITH? That's what nerf guns are FOR—*
> *so kids can go shoot kids, right? C'mon man, c'mon.*
> > *Dude, I used to have frickin BB WARS! Frickin go*
> > *grab your BB gun and some friends and*
> > *shoot at each other out in the—*
>
> *Your dad was a cop, right!?*
> > *Yeah yeah, career cop, Dad—HAHAHA—Dad used to be like:*
> > *no BB guns inside, you'll ding up the walls!*
> > *But he'd be all like: put on your winter coats*
> > *and these goggles, you know, eye protection,*
> > *just no head shots—HAHAHAHA*
> > > *—no head shots.*

And they will sigh and sigh, wipe their eyes,
lift ball caps and latch them back over foreheads,
already on to the next segment about
how Thursday is the new Friday.

> The policeman's son summons the elevator
> > (thinks he can feel it)

> glad he doesn't have to laugh on weekends
> > (the old gods growing tired
> > of holding down the calendar)

> orders a tank top with Kurt Cobain's suicide note
> printed on the front
> > (that the names he's known
> > in the past might not make
> > the future come when called)

finds the video called "5 Signs You're Reincarnated"
(won't really tell you

and the thunderstorm flavour on the air
won't make it past the patch of tongue
that tastes bitter).

A hunch will shudder in him,
some suspicion
scratching that dog spot
that makes a back leg
lift and twitch by its ear,
churn nothing,
sway on three feet,
shiver
like a jammed
reel-to-reel.

THERE ARE SOME KINDS OF WEALTH I WANT, AND SOME I DON'T
(OR: *THE ABYSMAL GLITZ ONE MIGHT ENCOUNTER WHILE FIXING THE AIR CONDITIONERS OF THE 1%)* (OR: *WHEN NOT TO DO THE MACARENA)*

They have an ensuite with twelve-foot ceilings
—one wall mirror, one wall marble—
and bathtub big enough for your tits and your knees
to be wet at the same time.

They have a serving tray
that looks like it's made of pressed flowers,
but look closer: each petal is a butterfly wing
guarded under glass. Down the hall,
a geode the size of artisanal sourdough
winks like a star-cloud on a teak end table.

They have a stuffed polar bear in one of the living rooms.
It rears on hind legs, paws forever stuck
in phase two of the Macarena,
as if it was shot during *Ice Breaker Hour*
at a corporate retreat.

They have a better view than the space station,
and small fleets of Range Rovers—
a Range Rover can get so lonely on its own.

And they have me. I climb into the guts of the place
wearing boots the government bought,
suck spider corpses out of their heat recovery ventilation units,
dribble sweat all over their expensive insulation
as I campaign across the attic joist by joist.

The ghosts of those spiders will remember this day.
Oh yes. They will remember this day as:
The Great Scourge Brought Down Upon Our Innocent Graves
by Tomb Raider Lucia and Her Shop Vac of Most Terrible Destruction.

70

I will remember it as the day I learned
how to service HRV units, and encountered my first
(and, so far, only) privately owned dead polar bear.

They will not remember it at all. Which is fine.
Surely their lives are occupied by other concerns
as they unspool in this lovely, lonely house, full
of beautiful things displayed on beautiful stands.
And ugly things. Displayed on beautiful stands.

THE AMERICAN DOLLAR

The portrait of Earth
that our teachers
lowered over the blackboard
lied to us.
Its lines have been tidied
in service of right angles,
forced straight long ago
so a sailor could chart
from port to port
without looking up
from his own compass.

By the first anniversary of 9/11,
we were bored of the war,
but it took a few more years
for someone to figure out
that if you fold a twenty
like a wingless paper airplane,
two towers show up in the pleat,
burning down the center.

To maintain the shapes of continents
our map must distort their size.
Greenland gets as much ink as Africa.
This is the price of unfolding
a round world onto a flat plane.

It was a fix, see? Just ask the money,
we'd joke, stroking the bill creaseless
once more on the resin bar top.
We could turn it into anything
we wanted: another round
of Greyhounds, globe citrus
and juniper in our blood
making sharp corners curve,
contorting whatever route
our tires burnt on the way home.

GOOSE THIEF

small woman in a stretched shirt
    striped like she's blown through a sticky curtain of the seventies
    like warm wine gums are drawn armpit to armpit across her chest
passes on Charles and snarls, mostly to me
get your own fucking music, you Jew

I wonder how she knows, my provenance
yes, but more so about the songs I've stolen:

        the car horns who scream at each other
        like beasts across a clearing

        the pocketed gosling
        singing under my sweater

        serrated tongue of the hard-beaked
        goose god in my mouth

        (his hisses are my dearest hatchets
        his croon a silver madrigal of blade)

NOBODY NOTATES THE BACK OF BAD PHOTOS
FOR THE FLEA MARKET BROWSER'S BENEFIT

Sixties, judging by the hairdos.
A wedding reception?

The bald man with the tie clip
and Masonic ring
wears a carnation in his left lapel.
He's caught in a blink, jaw lax.

Mother of the bride's mouth
is hooked, her cheeks
mean to drag smoke, but when
she blows it back, they'll soften.

Groomsman's left lid droops,
though he'll be handsome again
once the shutter shuts.

All the guests, suspended mid–
gesture, incomplete impulse, seem bored.

Back from the printer in its white border,
they will pass the photograph around
with the others: *My god,* they might think,
is that really what I look like?

ECHO PARK, SILVER LAKE, LOS FELIZ, FIGURE 8

Once the bar napkins are full of scribble and epiphany
funny hasty cock drawings and Oscar nominations

road soda blueprints that reach from bar to bar
what will you fold over and push toward

your friend between the highball glasses?
What will hold your exquisite corpse then?

Walk L.A. at 5 a.m., p.m., whatever, doesn't matter
every car going past sounds like a match

being struck against the side of your head.

                    Every car going past will match you:
                    5 a.m. reckless, *whatever, doesn't matter*

                    you're an exquisite corpse with a head held
                    high and round as a 76 sign, smudgy glass

                    torso from some other staggerer, folding over
                    the bottle who blueprinted your incongruous body

                    the hasty cocktail who scrawled these feet
                    dragging two scribbles down Sunset.

BOP IT, FLICK IT, TWIST IT, SPIN IT

Well, we really cocked that one up, didn't we?

We had one teat not to suckle raw
one scab not to pick
one bath not to poop
    and we pooped it.

Yup, we really popped the old waterbed
really tipped the big steamy bowl of ramen
into the collective lap.

We had one limo not to barf
    and we barfed it.
One cat not to shave
    and look who's all skin
    and hiss
    and piss-on-the-shoe-rack
    now.

We were fortunate:
    the recipients of all this wobbly hardware
    this noble momentum toward
    Why the hell not?

We were given so many thought tokens,
    won so many tickets at the Reason Arcade,
and we traded them in for so many Things:
    Bayonets and theremins and brain surgery and trench warfare!
    Industrious revolutions!
    Fetish nights and freighters!
    Church music and touch screens!
    Oil pours and soccer tournaments and happy fracking accidents!
    That Beyoncé polish on our shining seas!
    This Jay-Z suit jacket
    wrapped around our chilly prom-night shoulders
    like a hug that's richer than God!

And we have been happy
    as chinchillas
    in a Pompeii dust bath
clean and free
    as a ballsack
    in the last bathhouse.

But we really wiped back to front
before the big game
this time, didn't we?

Yup. We are the kind of scrotums
who bring pork chops to Piglet's potluck
    wings to Big Bird's birthday party
who bite the corners off all the samosas
    then put them back on the platter
    and are like, *Hey, guys, I brought samosas!*

We fucking hate that guy.

But we are that guy
who puts beef jerky in his breast pocket
    and goes on a walk to the dog park
    like nothing's gonna happen
who drives his Camaro into the river
    then swims back to the bar.

We really crossed a state line
    with a minor in the back seat
    this time, didn't we?
Really ran our fist into the wall
    beside her head
    when she spoke back.

We really carcinoma'd that canary
really scraped the sky bloody
bankrupted the glaciers
bit hard the tongue of writhing progress.

We really danced off our foot
    for the debt trap to gnaw on
really felled the last redwood

really stabbed the clouds
    really angry

really warred those bayonets
    really weary

really morphined the forest
this time, didn't we?

And now the empire is falling.

We never even looked up from the Bop-It
    to take in the view from the zenith.

Never stopped licking the ledgers
    long enough to find our own nipples.

We barely felt the fulcrum kick out
from under us
    pinned as we were
    under a comfortable Humvee
    swaddled in flammable blankets
    smoking cigars and feeling like ballers.

What a Rome.

What an old story.

What a short, short sight we were.

THROWOUT BEARING, DROP POCKET, AND HOW IT MAYBE HAPPENS

I. *Your Broken Wrist*

You were driving a screw, let's say into concrete.
Inch and a half, galvanized, sturdy shank.

The drill in your hand transferred the motor's spin
to the threads of the fastener,
kissed torque from trigger to chuck to bit to spiral tip.

Your drill—wedding gift from an older brother,
that one you managed to hold on to by hiding it
behind cans of paint thinner during the divorce—
had no clutch, no mechanism to sense resistance,
choke when the threshold was reached.

So when the head of the screw landed in the cement
and the motor's power met the immovable,
all its will bounced back into the tool,
throwing the handle counterclockwise
with the full fury of the thwarted.

And you, being you, were holding on too tight,
so your wrist splintered like a sheath of dry pasta
twisted between two fists.

Now pain braises your arm
when you open pickle jars,
and the Macarena has become an agony.

II. *Your Flattened Thumbnail*

You were shooting pool, let's say at the Legion.
Like anyone who spent hours of irretrievable youth
learning to slip movement from wrist to stick
to ball to ball to pocket,
you know the candied pleasure of the perfect shot,
the satisfaction smack, black planet darting away
to drop clean in a corner.

You bent, lined 'er up, gave a couple test thrusts,
and drove the cue as if to skewer that ball.
Then you, being you, turned,
leaned on the edge of the table
so sure you'd hear the smite, the sink.

But you missed. And that ball,
heavy as eight dollars in quarters,
met the edge at its own angle
and came careening back,
found your thumb
against the felt lip.
And all its speed was bequeathed into your flesh,
shook your vessels till they burst
like James Brown's heart onstage,
pushed their guts up on your thumbnail,
collapsed against it in their torn purple suits.

Now your nail bed is filled with blood,
pressure building
under its plum and motor-oil bruise.

III. *Your Unmourned Dead*

Hit by a train, say.

Taken by tumour.

Pulled through a planer of pain
on the twelfth floor of a downtown hospital.

Overdosed in Palo Alto
on a bedroom floor
immovable.

Now your heart grand-marshals the Parade of the Clobbered,
liver limps to bring up the rear.
Your bronchioles keep dropping the baton,
and your hands have ducked out of the marching band
to go puke in an alley.

That torment in your wrist?
That throb in your finger?
That grief you feel
dicing the tender inside of your elbow
and sliding its hunting knife between your toes?

It is the recoil of power
caught in your body.

STEPS I HAVE TAKEN
WITH ONE HAND HOLDING THE DOOR CLOSED,
WARY OF GRATITUDE AND OTHER SNAKE OILS

Signed for the thousand boxes Loss delivers
to the doorstep of the living. Refused their work.
Didn't open, unpack, collapse.

Hung the punching bag, pulled the blinds
and cracked another Kokanee, its aluminum lip
the only altar sharp enough to accept such wary prayer.

Cut my knuckle deep on the recent parting.
Blood, thin and eager to spring its vessels and be free
from the task of filling me, didn't run but sprinted.

Didn't get tattooed. Didn't get lost. Didn't lose it at the ladies
who asked if it had been the drugs. Not when the answer was yes.
Not when it was no. Didn't refuse to return from the trip.

Chased a child down a corridor on all fours,
fast enough to threaten but never quite to catch,
the way I used to think death moves.

Climbed twelve storeys of St. Paul's. On each landing
passed an apostle, patrons of stairwells and hallways
waiting patient for floors to pace.

Stroked the nettle coat of the creature who is sent out
to collect reluctant supplicants. Braided three names into its mane.
Gave it three new shoes. Sent it back to its farrier limping.

REFORMATION

I had some habits that could've been called prayer,
back before I deboned my own tarot, stopped believing myself
part of a symbology. It is better, not to beg Pain for so much
meaning, not to let it boil into a vial of holy blood.

Better, to convert the reliquary to a home office
and only light candles when the power goes out.
To write dismissive jokes on my palms,
keep them from ever
quite meeting.

AFTER EVERY FUNERAL

I lay my watch at the sink's lip,
pull off my rings,
slide teeth from teeth
and step from my undone
dress into the tub.

Work a scouring pad
across the enamel,
my breasts pressed
to my knees.

I am not innocent
to this methodical need
to scrub to scrape to sweep
at expanses that have
nothing to express.

The watch by the sink
strides with my strokes.

Its hands in the mirror
tell a time it is not.

The earrings I wore
to the service
knock at my jaw
as I clean.

It doesn't matter
that the tub was dirty
or that it will not be.
This is frank work
with no end
except to move
one surface across another.

RECESSION

We drive to the actual ocean
two days after the memorial.
Stop in Qualicum for fish and chips,
the strait blue, black Sharpies in both our pockets.

We're tagging our dead friend's shape
across the island, trying to fasten
a broken bracelet back around the world's radius.

Slowed to the pace of ritual, the trip takes years.

In Tofino, we find a timber-frame house where two dogs live.
One has a coat like mottled sea storm, digs at the beach,
throws his head in the sand to sniff for blood worms.

The other is tweaked and peaceless
with an unceasing need to retrieve.

She arrives and arrives with some tiny token
—half a crayon, wrapper off a juice-box straw, a bead—
to drop at our feet, whines and pulls her eyes back
to the whites until we throw it.
And then again. Again.
When I have to go to bed, she tries to follow me
with a piece of onion skin in her mouth.

I would stay longer
if she wasn't still at my door
in the morning, a pile of charms between her paws.

Instead, I leave that town—like all towns—
retreating along its two-lane highway,
the asphalt lip of ocean and the asphalt lip of sky
the asphalt lip of elsewhere and the asphalt lip of here,
pressed together and humming.

LISTENING AGAIN TO MAURICE SENDAK
INTERVIEWED SHORTLY BEFORE HIS DEATH

Live your life, live your life, live your life,
he pleads, as always, in tears at the end.

I imagine him, an old man
alone in his house, one hand
stroking the head of his last cat.

I cry a lot because I miss people.

He sits, on the phone with the radio host,
in a desk chair rolled up to the window.

The maple tree outside washes shadow
across the room—books and letters
stacked askew on the oak table,

a butterprint bowl by the sink
where his griefs soak like dried beans.

They die and I can't stop them.
They leave me and I love them more.

My grief is something small and sharp
I stepped on barefoot. A fragment
of broken dish deep in my heel.

live your life live your life live your life

Said aloud it sounds like a running tap.

LUMINA

A dead wasp on the tennis court
catches me as I walk back to my jacket,
racquet swinging from one finger.

I crouch to look closer.
Its wing is a lattice of veins too small
to imagine hollow, too fine to be empty,

body bright on the blue cement
that the city will paint deep green
during rain season.

Its eye is the last drop of ink
flicked from a dry fountain pen.

It has no feel between my fingers,
no weight as I set it in my hand.
Look away, I am holding nothing.

Still, it is dangerous, a blaze
on my skin, hot velvet in my palm,
and I flinch when the wind turns it over.

I FIND MYSELF ILLITERATE IN ANY LANGUAGE THAT MIGHT EXPLAIN ME

a wood shop strewn with cigarette butts

the hazmat situation in my liver

drawers full of Life Savers, hospital socks

estate sale portraiture

or the inlet,
    on an all-grey day from Jericho
    pebbles, tankers
    too beautiful to be alone with

my gentle body
    who has been
    in every moment

    so unheard
    she's stopped throbbing
    under certain songs

    disguises her half
    of the diary
    in cracking hips

every pang is the same:
    an invitation sent collect

    the pile-up of daily voices
    asking if I'll accept
    the charges

THE PROBLEM WITH BEING A BOX
TOO SMALL FOR ITS CONTENTS

Love, you ask too many questions.
Let's agree: we are whole

—John Thompson, "Ghazal II"

I take apart the watch
you left here
a thousand times each day.
It does not help me
understand time.

I press our mirrors together
as if I could pin the infinite
but the glass
will not be rasped
back to sand.

I try to sift
the love from grief
the grief from love
and only succeed
in splitting my own atom.

Still, my body refuses to part with me
insists that we are an ever-changing entirety
declines to debate me on this fact

as I twist and spit
mind scalpelling
itself to bits
a vivisectionist bent
over a strapped animal
muttering
    find peace
    find peace
as she works.

And indivisible
under her knife
the reply:

there is no love
without the first love

one's own
lost love

may you rejoin yourselves

may you survive
even when you don't want to.

WHAT MAKES ME JEALOUS OF THE FALCON WHO LIVES OUT BY THE LANDFILL?

Not the storm she swallows
on the thermals, not its edge
reflected in her eye
or the rain that whets her beak,
her polished claws.

But how she slows her dive by opening
from missile to mainsail,
admits her belly to the wind

tips against her own momentum

to coronate a telephone pole,
settle like a crown on the mast
by which so many voices travel.

How she tucks away her wings,
rests her body in her body
and when she is ready, calls out,
her cry a cloud with no one else's sky behind it.

ACKNOWLEDGMENTS

The poems in this book were imagined, written and revised on the unceded territory of the Musqueam, Squamish and Tsleil-Waututh people. Like me, they reside on the stolen land of those First Nations.

An earlier version of "In Event Of Moon Disaster" appeared in *Alive At The Center: Contemporary Poems from the Pacific Northwest* (Ooligan Press, 2013). Thank you to the editors of that anthology for its inclusion.

to Erin Kirsh, for her immense help and incessant encouragement, and for being my favourite flavour of triple threat: brilliant, thoughtful and seemingly never asleep.

to Jillian Christmas, whose years of support, inspiration, luminance and love have helped both this book and its author find their way through the mirror maze.

to Ryan Rainey, who—among a million other kindnesses—never said no when I asked if he'd listen to one more poem, "just real fast, before you go to bed."

to my sister Nina and our parents, Victoria and Tony, who are not only *in* my corner, but are the corner itself.

to Julia, who showed me that there's nothing wrong with us.

to Elaine, who has helped hold it together the whole time.

to Alessandra Naccarato and Brad Morden at Write Bloody North, the best godparents a first collection could ask for.

to Brendan, Mono, Josie, RC, Johnny, Ben, Duncan, Barbara, Robert and Ian, for the time, insight, and excellent advice regarding these poems and poetry in general.

to all the friends who have likewise nurtured this book by seeing to my care and feeding during its creation; you know who you are, and so do I, and I love you.

to Mike, Dave and Geoff, for lighting the fuse in the first place.

and to Zaccheus, to Pam, and to Daphne, who are not gone, so much as everywhere.

Thank you.

NOTES

Please read these poems aloud, if you can. They want to hear themselves in your voice.

The epigraph to "Digestion Begins In The Mouth" is from a 2017 interview with Rachael Denhollander, the lawyer, author and former gymnast who was the first person to publicly accuse former USA Gymnastics doctor Larry Nassar of sexual assault. She was eventually joined by more than two hundred other women and girls.

The quotations in "Listening Again To Maurice Sendak Interviewed Shortly Before His Death" are drawn from an interview recorded in September 2011 with Terry Gross for the NPR program *Fresh Air*.

Cicatrices is the plural of *cicatrix*, which means the scar of a healed wound. In botany, the term refers to the mark left on a plant when a leaf or branch has become detached.

"In Event Of Moon Disaster" takes its name and inspiration from William Safire's 1969 contingency speech written for President Nixon to deliver in case the Apollo 11 astronauts were stranded on the lunar surface with no hope of rescue.

Lumina is the plural of *lumen*, which in Latin means *an opening*. The word can refer to the unit of light emitted by a single candle, or in biology, to the empty space inside a vessel or organ.

ABOUT THE AUTHOR

LUCIA MISCH is a writer, performer and facilitator. She can be found on stages across North America, from literary festivals to labour union conventions to local poetry shows, and her writing has been published in print and online. As a teaching artist, Lucia is dedicated to helping others—especially youth—inhabit their creative, personal and political power through writing.

Lucia grew up at an astronomical observatory in the foothills east of San José and currently lives on unceded Musqueam, Squamish and Tsleil-Waututh territory in Vancouver. *The Problem with Solitaire* is her debut collection.

www.luciamisch.com

Write Bloody North publishes groundbreaking voices and legends of spoken word
to create innovative, fresh poetry books. A new voice in Canadian publishing, we are
an independent imprint of the trail-blazing Write Bloody Publishing (Los Angeles).
Beautiful, Canadian-made books.

Want to know more about Write Bloody North books, authors, and events?
Join our mailing list at

www.writebloody.com